PRACTICAL RESPONSES TO REAL PROBLEMS

EIGHT POVERTY REDUCTION CASES FROM THE ASIAN DEVELOPMENT BANK

VOLUME 2

JULY 2022

ASIAN DEVELOPMENT BANK

© 2022 Asian Development Bank
6 ADB Avenue, Mandaluyong City, 1550 Metro Manila, Philippines
Tel +63 2 8632 4444; Fax +63 2 8636 2444
www.adb.org

Some rights reserved. Published in 2022.

ISBN 978-92-9269-609-2 (print); 978-92-9269-610-8 (electronic); 978-92-9269-611-5 (ebook)
Publication Stock No. SPR220278-2
DOI: http://dx.doi.org/10.22617/SPR220278-2

The views expressed in this publication are those of the authors and do not necessarily reflect the views and policies of the Asian Development Bank (ADB) or its Board of Governors or the governments they represent.

ADB does not guarantee the accuracy of the data included in this publication and accepts no responsibility for any consequence of their use. The mention of specific companies or products of manufacturers does not imply that they are endorsed or recommended by ADB in preference to others of a similar nature that are not mentioned.

By making any designation of or reference to a particular territory or geographic area, or by using the term "country" in this document, ADB does not intend to make any judgments as to the legal or other status of any territory or area.

Please contact pubsmarketing@adb.org if you have questions or comments with respect to content, or if you wish to obtain copyright permission for your intended use that does not fall within these terms, or for permission to use the ADB logo.

Corrigenda to ADB publications may be found at http://www.adb.org/publications/corrigenda.

Notes:
In this publication, "$" refers to United States dollars, "A$" refers to Australian dollars, "CNY" refers to Chinese yuan, "NRs" refers to Nepalese rupees, "PRs" refers to Pakistani rupees, and "Tk" refers to Bangladeshi taka.
ADB recognizes "China" as the People's Republic of China.

Cover design by Francis Manio.

CONTENTS

FOREWORD

As economies in Asia and the Pacific reach middle-income status, millions are lifted out of poverty. However, critical development challenges remain. On top of these challenges is the coronavirus disease (COVID-19) pandemic that has led to unprecedented disruptions in all facets of life. Financing, knowledge, and partnerships help the Asian Development Bank (ADB) work with its developing member countries (DMCs) to meet these challenges. Lessons learned in fighting the pandemic have underlined the importance of knowledge sharing across sectors, cultures, and systems.

Building on the successful knowledge shared from the first volume in November 2019, this second volume showcases more innovative projects that have been effective in reducing poverty. As with the first volume, these projects in the form of brief case studies demonstrate how ADB has worked with its DMCs to address their development challenges—this time with greater emphasis on stories from the beneficiaries themselves.

The four themes of this publication—ensuring equality and inclusion, caring for the environment, securing food for all, and sustaining prosperity through access to finance—illustrate how ADB strives to help its DMCs holistically. Stories from India and Pakistan, for example, show how the building and rehabilitation of rural roads helped foster inclusion, especially for women and children. Innovative energy projects in the Cook Islands and the People's Republic of China not only provided connectivity—they also ensured environmental sustainability.

These case studies show evidence of the impact of ADB's interventions and illustrate how lessons learned can be applied to reduce poverty in other parts of Asia and the Pacific region.

Amid ongoing challenges and global changes, ADB will continue to share knowledge with DMCs to help transform and build a resilient and sustainable poverty-free future.

Ahmed Saeed
Vice-President (Operations 2)
East Asia, Southeast Asia, and the Pacific
Asian Development Bank

ACKNOWLEDGMENTS

This publication was produced by the Asian Development Bank (ADB) through the collective efforts of staff members from four regional departments—Central and West Asia, East Asia, South Asia, and the Pacific.

Eight project case studies were initially collected from the regional departments and submitted as part of the Second Global Call of Best Poverty Reduction Practices organized by the International Poverty of Reduction Center in China together with six other international organizations in 2020. ADB's effort was led by ADB–the People's Republic of China Regional Knowledge Sharing Initiative (RKSI), East Asia Department.

The support of the ADB management, particularly ADB Vice-President (Operations 2) Ahmed Saeed, and M. Teresa Kho, director general of the East Asia Department are acknowledged. We thank Kenichi Yokoyama, director general of the South Asia Department; Eugenue Zhukov, director general of the Central and West Asia Department; Leah Gutierrez, director general of the Pacific Department; and Bruno Carrasco, director general of the Sustainable Development and Climate Change Department for their cooperation and support. Hsiao Chink Tang, senior economist, RKSI, led the study, and edited and supervised the production of the publication.

We would like to sincerely thank the writers of the case studies, who also acted as peer reviewers: Zhiming Niu and Lanlan Lu of the East Asia Department; Nasheeba Selim and Suman Subba of the South Asia Department; Khuram Imtiaz Butt of the Central and West Asia Department; Matthew Hodge and Eun Young So of the Pacific Department; and Prabhjot Khan of the Sustainable Development and Climate Change Department. The publication would not have been possible without their excellent effort that ensures the work is accessible to the widest audience possible.

Several others deserve thanks for their valuable help. Dan Wang coordinated the publication production. Prince Nicdao did the layout and typesetting.

Finally, we appreciate the support of the Department of Communications in publishing the publication.

ABBREVIATIONS

ADB	–	Asian Development Bank
CEFPF	–	Clean Energy Fund under the Clean Energy Financing Partnership Facility
DAE	–	Department of Agricultural Extension, Bangladesh
DCH	–	data clearinghouse
DOLIDAR	–	Department of Local Infrastructure Development and Agricultural Roads, Nepal
FFS	–	farmer field school
GDP	–	gross domestic product
ha	–	hectare
HKP	–	Haveli, Kotli, and Poonch, Pakistan
HVC	–	high-value crop
km	–	kilometer
km^2	–	square kilometer
kWh	–	kilowatt-hour
m^3	–	cubic meter
MFI	–	microfinance institution
MHVRA	–	multi-hazard vulnerability risk assessment
MLBGPs	–	medium and large-sized biogas plants
MSEs	–	micro and small enterprises
MW	–	megawatt
MWh	–	megawatt-hour
NGO	–	nongovernment organization
PNG	–	Papua New Guinea
PRC	–	People's Republic of China
TOT	–	training-of-trainers

OVERVIEW

Background

Recent setbacks to poverty alleviation because of the coronavirus disease (COVID-19) pandemic underscore the urgency to deepen efforts to reduce poverty and inequality. ADB estimates show more than 75 to 80 million people went into extreme poverty in developing Asia in 2020 because of the pandemic (ADB 2021). While the recovery is under way in developing Asia, it is still largely incomplete in most of the region. Since the outbreak began, the Asian Development Bank (ADB) has been helping its developing members respond through finance, partnerships, and knowledge sharing.

This publication shares ADB's knowledge through case studies of recent ADB poverty reduction projects in Bangladesh, the People's Republic of China (PRC), the Cook Islands, India, Nepal, Pakistan, and Papua New Guinea. The case studies highlight innovative interventions and effective approaches to reduce poverty by ensuring equality and inclusion, caring for the environment, securing food for all, and sustaining prosperity through access to finance. The publication builds on the first volume and shares innovative experiences gained from the projects' success.

Ensuring Equality and Inclusion

High on ADB's agenda is ensuring human development and social inclusion, quality jobs, education and training, better health, and social protection. Accomplishing these goals requires scaling up support for gender equality in human development, decision-making, and leadership; empowering women economically; reducing women's time poverty; and strengthening women's resilience to shocks.

Two projects highlight equality and inclusion. A rural connectivity program in India resulted in higher agricultural production, better cropping patterns, safe mobility, and socioeconomic opportunities for women and girls, and women's greater self-esteem and leadership capacity. A flood emergency reconstruction and resilience project in Pakistan reduced travel time, improved road safety, and promoted economic and social recovery by expanding the delivery of health, education, and food security.

Caring for Our Environment

Ensuring low greenhouse gas emissions, an improved approach to building climate and disaster resilience, environmental sustainability, and strengthening livelihood and energy security have helped reduce poverty in Asia and the Pacific. The Poverty Reduction through Renewable Energy Project in the Cook Islands, which is still being implemented, has promoted energy efficiency and renewable energy, increased access to energy for all, and implemented reforms to build local capacity and support sector governance. Through the project, electricity tariffs and oil imports have been reduced, and electricity supply has become more reliable—improving living conditions and giving rise to new livelihood opportunities.

An innovative project in the PRC—the Integrated Biogas Renewable Energy— improved rural livelihoods by converting livestock waste into biogas renewable energy and eco-farming products.

Securing Food for All

To secure food for all, market connectivity and agricultural value-chain linkages, agricultural productivity, and food safety are considered essential. In the PRC, an agricultural development project in Ningxia Hui Autonomous Region demonstrated that an integrated management approach was able to improve local farmers' livelihoods and food security while protecting the ecology. In Bangladesh, the Second Crop Diversification Project increased landownership among women farmers—from 51% to 70%— and empowered them. It also significantly improved beneficiaries' food intake and their patterns of food consumption.

Sustaining Prosperity through Access to Finance

In Papua New Guinea, financial sustainability, service delivery, capacity, and standards were improved through a microfinance expansion project. The project provided microfinance services, financial literacy, and business development skills training; and increased the number of loan and savings accounts. In Nepal, a project sought to reduce poverty in conflict-affected communities—in 18 hill and mountain districts—by constructing and rehabilitating roads and bridges, training disadvantaged groups in livelihood skills, and connecting them to microfinance institutions.

All these projects aimed for inclusive development—to leave no one behind.

ENSURING EQUALITY AND INCLUSION

2

INDIA: PAVING THE WAY TO PROGRESS
Rural Connectivity Investment Program Project 1

→ 1,787 rural households benefited from 3,782 kilometers of newly constructed roads
→ 197,160 road construction jobs opened

PAKISTAN: STAYING BUOYANT THROUGH RESILIENCE
Flood Emergency Reconstruction and Resilience Project

→ 1,158 hectares of land stabilized through bioengineering
→ 120 to 150 years of flood embankment life expected with the use of sheet piling

▶ 2.1   INDIA: PAVING WAY TO PROGRESS
Rural Connectivity Investment Program Project 1

Abstract

The Rural Connectivity Investment Program of ADB, approved in 2012 for $252 million, aimed to help India's national rural roads program—*Pradhan Mantri Gram Sadak Yojana*—in Assam, Chhattisgarh, Madhya Pradesh, Odisha, and West Bengal. At project completion, 3,782 kilometers (km) of rural roads were constructed, benefiting 1,787 rural households, of whom 46% were vulnerable and 10% were headed by females. Women comprised 37% of road construction workers and 44% of road maintenance workers receiving equal pay for work of equal value. Women also influenced the road alignment and the grievance redressal committees. Overall, the improved rural road network resulted in higher agricultural production, better cropping patterns, safe mobility, and socioeconomic opportunities for women and girls, and enhanced self-esteem and leadership capacities of women.

Background

Life was difficult for 1,600 rural households in the Indian states of Assam, Chhattisgarh, Madhya Pradesh, Odisha, and West Bengal. Lack of rural connectivity deprived households of various socioeconomic and financial benefits. Women were particularly affected as most economic sectors were dominated by men. Without proper roads, they could not find proper jobs and adequately access social infrastructure, development schemes, and health-care benefits such as *anganwadis* or childcare centers.

On occasions, they also could not fully capitalize on incentives aimed to help them. For example, although girls enrolled in high schools were given free bicycles in some states, they could not use

Project at a Glance	
Rural Connectivity Investment Program Project 1	
Approved:	22 August 2012
Closed:	2 January 2019
Project Cost:	

• **Asian Development Bank**
  $252 million

Executing Agency:
  Ministry of Rural Development, India

them to travel to schools. "I, along with my friends, could not pursue our high school studies because the senior high school was far from our village, and our parents would not permit us to travel far," said Diksha Pandey of Sira Village in Madhya Pradesh.

Interventions

In 2012, ADB responded to the Government of India's request by constructing and upgrading priority rural roads to all-weather roads in the five states (ADB 2012b). The project included numerous features that promoted women's economic empowerment by creating opportunities for their engagement in skilled and unskilled road construction and maintenance work. These included (i) special mitigation measures for vulnerable households headed by females; (ii) women's participation in project planning (road alignment) and village grievance redressal committees (VGRCs); (iii) "friendly" road design features that took into consideration the elderly, children, women, and people with disabilities; (iv) socially inclusive and gender-responsive training materials; (v) women's participation in technical and nontechnical rural road capacity development initiatives; (vi) capacity building of project stakeholders (staff of project implementing units, elected representatives, contractors, and project consultants) in gender mainstreaming in rural road projects; and (vii) project monitoring mechanisms that collected sex-disaggregated data and captured and reported project gender equality and women's empowerment results.

Results

First, new and better roads improved connectivity and mobility. Surpassing the project's original target of 3,461 km, 3,782 km of all-weather rural roads were constructed. This benefited 1,787 rural households (against the target of 1,600), of whom 46% were vulnerable households and 10% were households headed by females. Women beneficiaries highlighted benefits such as safe mobility, and improved access to development programs and services, including access to reproductive health-care services and children's easier travel to schools (ADB 2019a, ADB 2020a).

"The project built roads from our village to the Gram Panchayat (village council) where the high school is located. This reignited our dream of higher education. We can now use our bicycles to reach school without any difficulty," added Diksha Pandey.

The improved roads also allayed fears of parents. This made them more ready to let their daughters enroll in higher grades. "Life has changed for the girls who want to spread their wings and live their dreams, all thanks to the newly constructed road," she said. The women also described that the improved connectivity helped reduce their poverty, afforded them more work, and improved services in their communities.

Second, women were empowered. A total of 197,160 (37% women) worked in road construction and 36,735 (44% women) worked in road maintenance. All the project states reported 100% compliance with labor laws. The project included gender-related provisions

such as engagement of women, equal pay for work of equal value, and child labor prohibition. Women's representation in VGRCs helped them to influence road design and alignments, resolve complaints, and participate in community road construction and maintenance.

"We are women VGRC members in block Balikuda, Odisha," shared Anita Malik, and a few other women in Odisha. "In our habitation, the 6.5 km road in Ramtola village was expected to benefit 1,392 villagers. However, the construction was stalled because the private landowners refused to give up their land." As the demand for the road was gaining momentum, especially among poor village women, a VGRC was formed with 35% women members to persuade the landowners. "We mobilized women's support and negotiated with the landowners. In the end we succeeded by employing our collective voice. The resolution was passed, and the road was constructed," Anita continued.

Rural roads have enabled girls' access to education by promoting independent mobility (photo by ADB).

Third, poverty and deprivation were reduced, and jobs created. The improved road connectivity boosted the income of households engaged in farming, and various other services. It facilitated access to markets and main areas of economic activity, which in turn expanded job opportunities. Village women formed self-help groups and were involved in dairy farming. Milk collection and supply became easier with the use of auto-rickshaws and vans made possible by better roads. The groups supplied around 200 liters of milk every day to Puri, a popular religious hub in Odisha. Being a perishable commodity, better roads meant more timely delivery of milk, which ensured a steadier stream of income and business to the groups.

Rehana Begum, a widow, was another project beneficiary. The project helped her to access the main market. She was part of a self-help group and benefited from several development schemes. Her daughter was gifted a bicycle in school, which Rehana also used to transport vegetables. The road helped expand her horizons. She became not just an agricultural worker, but a businessperson.

Fourth, gender equality in the male-dominated transport sector was improved. There was a perceptible shift in the participation of female workers from casual workers in sericulture to producers and managers. The Rural Connectivity Training and Research Centers (RCTRCs) used socially inclusive and gender-responsive training methods and approaches. In all, 12% of women staff participated in 119 training events organized in the five RCTRCs. Gender and social safeguard trainings formed part of the training curriculum in these centers.

The RCTRCs infrastructure was gender-responsive and complied with the needs of people with disabilities. To facilitate women's participation in trainings, special hostel facilities were also provided. Project implementation units in Tikamgarh, Jabalpur, and Vidisha in Madhya

Pradesh deployed female junior engineers in the field, challenging traditional gender norms and stereotypes. This created a ripple effect whereby female community participation in awareness programs increased manifold due to the presence of female field staff. Women in villages felt less inhibited to participate in meetings, which traditionally were attended by men.

Finally, measures to help vulnerable female-headed households were provided. About 865 vulnerable households and those headed by females were linked to central- and state-funded development programs related to poverty reduction, social security, and economic empowerment.

Lessons

Overall, improved connectivity benefited project beneficiaries in terms of better job opportunities, higher income, and improved livelihood which all helped alleviate poverty. For example, farmers were able to access markets even during monsoons. Communities living in spatially disadvantaged areas could now access health facilities and services. Government service provisions such as water connection, electricity, and gas cylinder used for cooking became easier.

The implementation of the social and gender actions provided direct benefits through female participation in the workforce, human capital development, vulnerable and gender-responsive infrastructure design, and decision-making. It also resulted in institutional capacity building. Some of the factors that contributed to the efficient and effective delivery of gender action plan activities and the achievement of gender equality results are as follows:

- **Efficient monitoring system.** The National Rural Infrastructure Development Agency regularly monitored progress and achievements of the project's social and gender actions. Quantitative data across each activity were carefully monitored, stored, and managed. Beneficiary data were sex-disaggregated. Reports were supplemented with analytical excerpts, photographs, and documentary evidence.

- **Capacity development.** The RCTRCs took steps to ensure that (i) female participation in training programs was encouraged; (ii) data on training participants were sex-disaggregated; (iii) social inclusion and gender-responsive elements were included in the training modules; and (iv) social inclusion, gender equality, and social and environment safeguard sessions were mainstreamed in routine training events.

- **Institutional measures to promote gender equality.** To effectively monitor social and gender action implementation and oversight, gender focal points were designated at each project implementation unit.

- **Social safeguards and gender action implementation practices.** Each project state adopted innovative strategies and good practices for efficient and effective implementation, monitoring, reporting, and gender capacity development. A compendium of these good practices to enable cross-learning and replication will be a value addition toward social inclusion and gender mainstreaming goals in the transport sector.

2.2   PAKISTAN: STAYING BUOYANT THROUGH RESILIENCE
Flood Emergency Reconstruction and Resilience Project

Abstract

ADB approved the Flood Emergency
Reconstruction and Resilience Project in
September 2014 for $218.04 million, with
a $2 million technical assistance grant, in
response to floods in Pakistan. The project
(i) reconstructed and repaired 2,315 km
of provincial and district roads in Punjab;
(ii) reconstructed 203 km of major roads,
and repaired 66 km of district roads in Haveli,
Kotli, and Poonch (HKP); (iii) constructed a
bridge (160.7-meter span) on River Poonch;
(iv) stabilized 1,158 hectares (ha) of landslides in
HKP through bioengineering; and (v) rehabilitated
387 km of flood protection embankments in
Punjab, and constructed two new embankments
(7 km) on river Jhelum that protected the
cities of Jhelum (left bank) and Sarai Alamgir
(right bank). The innovative use of sheeting piling
in flood protection works enhanced expected
infrastructure life to 120–150 years. The project
resulted in improved connectivity and road
safety; increased income, particularly of women;
and reduction of poverty for the people in the
HKP region.

Background

A late and concentrated monsoon devastated
Pakistan in September 2014. This resulted in
flooding in the northern regions of Pakistan,
Punjab, and Sindh that affected 44 districts
and displaced more than 2.5 million people.
"My nursery was severely damaged during the
floods. I lost plants worth PRs3.1 million," said
the 31-year-old Saira Illyas, one of the Pakistan
Forest Department's guided nursery owners.

The flood caused 367 deaths and injured more
than 600 people in Punjab. Nearly 110,000

Project at a Glance		
Flood Emergency Reconstruction and Resilience Project		
Approved:	30 June 2015	
Closed:	30 April 2019	
Project Cost:		

• **Asian Development Bank**
  $218.04 million

Implementing Agencies:
Planning and development departments;
communication and works departments; Punjab
Irrigation Department; Punjab Disaster Management
Authority; Forest Department for the districts of
Haveli, Kotli, and Poonch

houses were destroyed or partially damaged.
More than 445,154 ha of agricultural land
was damaged, affecting 250,000 farmers and
resulting in the loss of standing food, fodder, and
cash crops. Nonfarm sources of livelihoods and
services were also affected, including many small,
manufacturing, and processing businesses.

Interventions

ADB responded by helping to restore and
reconstruct critical public and social
infrastructure to multi-hazard resilience
standards (ADB 2015b). These included
(i) reconstructing flood-damaged roads and
bridges in Punjab and the districts of HKP,
(ii) implementing flood-resilient irrigation and
flood management infrastructure in Punjab,
and (iii) strengthening disaster response and
management in the affected areas.

First, more than 2,300 km of roads were
reconstructed and rehabilitated in 21 flood-

■ A woman carries water from a reservoir using a walk path built by the project on the local women's request (photo by Muzaffar Bukhari).

affected districts of Punjab. Major arterial roads of over 200 km with safety measures friendly to women, children, and the elderly were rehabilitated. Connectivity was ensured through the repair of 66 km of damaged inter-district roads, and the construction of a 160-meter span bridge on the Poonch River.

Second, the project implemented various innovative flood irrigation and flood-resilient infrastructures. Sheet piling, the first in Pakistan, was used in flood embankments to ensure the structure's long life (120–150 years). Altogether 397 km of flood protection embankments were rehabilitated and/or upgraded, and 7 km of new embankments were constructed in Punjab. Given its high cost, sheet piling was only used in critical areas of the embankments, where any possible breach would cause irreparable losses.

Biological and engineering control measures were used to avoid landslides. These included layering and fencing with live hedges and live-staking; soft gabion walls/check-dams; vegetated loose-stone walls, loose-stone masonry works; earth works and galvanized iron wire-mesh gabions structures; and dibbling, sowing, and planting. Altogether 1,158 ha, against a target of only 200 ha, were stabilized.

In the past, falling boulders and debris from landslides caused many road accidents. In 2008, Syeeda Shamim Akhter's husband Syed Rashid Ahmed Shah lost his hand in a road accident. This left the family with no recourse but to request their eldest son to help out with the family expenses. To support his family, their eldest son left his studies and started working as a driver.

Third, the project strengthened the areas' disaster response and management. The Climate Change Center was established to develop a climate change policy that included sector plans, strategy, and road map for its implementation. The center, acting as the government's technical arm, would also review and appraise project proposals of line departments from a climate change mitigation and adaptation perspective.

Multi-hazard vulnerability risk assessments were carried out on the 20 most vulnerable districts of riverine floods in Punjab to help prepare more resilient projects. The results from these risk assessments were hosted in a data clearing house established at the Planning and Development Board, Punjab.

Manuals for safety inspection of dams and hydraulic structures were developed for the Health and Safety Unit of the Punjab Irrigation Department. A disaster risk management training course was also developed and adopted by the Engineering Academy of the Punjab Irrigation Department.

Results

With improved and safer roads, travel time was reduced. More vehicles could traverse the rehabilitated roads. Vehicle maintenance expenditure fell due to better road conditions resulting in saving to the owners. Road accidents also fell, making traveling safer.

Tourism picked up, contributing increased economic activity in HKP. The roads improvements in HKP pass through attractive and scenic environments such as lush green valleys, dense forests, noisy streams and waterfalls, and high passes.

Landslide stabilizations stood the test of severe weather. In 2019, despite the above normal monsoon season, heavy rains, and snowfall in the last winter, landslides did not happen. As a result, the government mandated that bioengineering measures be incorporated in slope stabilization of all road construction and rehabilitation projects in HKP and other districts in the region.

The well-being of local women and their families improved as their nursery business grew. Owners

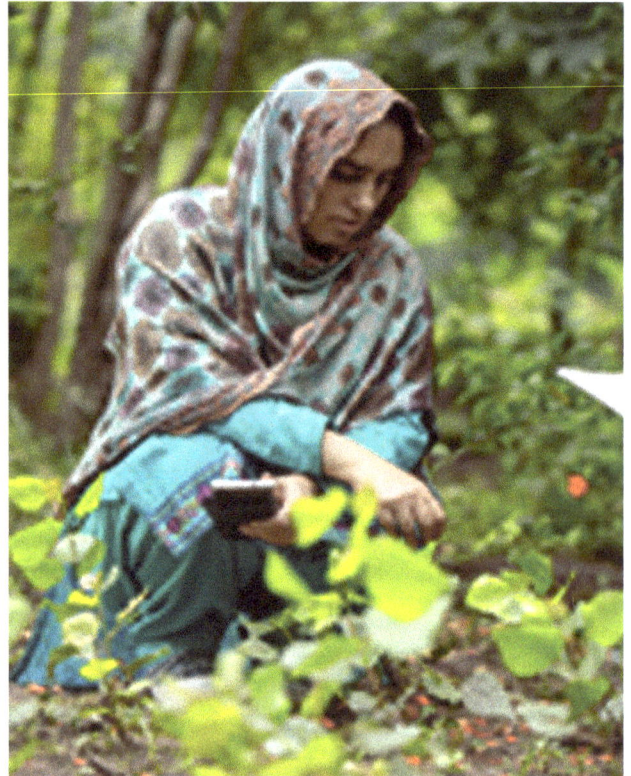

■ Saira Illiyas in her nursery (photo by Muzaffar Bukhari)..

of inactive nurseries also restarted their business. The government directed the Forest Department to procure saplings—planted on the landslide areas—preferably from women-owned nurseries. This ensured the sustainability of women's role in their business and the protection of treated landslides. Altogether the project bought plants from 24 nurseries, of which 15 (63%) were owned by women—against a target of 30%. The women nursery owners earned PRs23.3 million (about $150,000).

"During the last 3 years, I supplied about 7.2 hundred thousand plants to the Forest Departments of Poonch and Haveli districts and earned PRs8.8 million, which is quite a lot. This allowed me to expand my nursery from 40 to 70 kanals[1] and create additional 15 seasonal jobs for others. Now we own a house and a buffalo," added Saira Illyas.

[1] A kanal is a unit of area that equals 605 square yards.

Women's well-being also improved through various safety and facilitation measures implemented to address their concerns. "Thank you for protecting water reservoir and constructing staircase to safely access the reservoir. About 25 to 30 houses, shops, and a hotel in the vicinity are benefiting from this initiative," said 45-year-old Fahmeeda Jahan, resident of Bailan village on Azad Pattan-Rawalakot Road, while collecting water from the reservoir.

"We collect water 4 to 5 times in a day and spend 3 to 4 hours in fetching water. Not only has it enabled us to collect clean water, as previously during rainy season water was contaminated, but also saved our time and reduced injuries caused when the *katcha* track becomes slippery, causing injuries. Before, by sunset, it was not safe to fetch water." she added.

The upgraded flood embankments in Punjab helped protect infrastructure, agriculture land, and population from flooding. The use of sheet piling in nine flood embankments at critical sites provided adequate and long-term safety against any seepage of floodwater. The protection of agricultural land contributed to higher production and farmers' income, and reduced flood-induced damages to residential assets and agriculture crops.

With the setting up of the Climate Change Center, HKP and its adjoining regions were able to integrate climate change mitigation and adaptation measures into development planning across all sectors.

Strengthening of early warning systems, predictive simulation modeling, and flood plain physical modeling enabled the provincial and district government to control disasters in a more effective manner and minimize economic losses. Results of the risk assessments were integrated in the data clearing house and accessible by all line departments. The risk assessment studies collected a complete socioeconomic and gender-disaggregated data of 1.1 million households with 6 million population. An application dashboard allowed users to select the best site for their proposed development projects, keeping in view identified risks and vulnerability to various hazards prevailing in the area. The dashboard could also be used to estimate economic losses helping authorities to make more informed decisions.

Lessons Learned

The project highlighted the importance of women's involvement in project design and implementation. These provided economic opportunities to a large segment of the society, and contributed to reduced poverty. Women's active role led to a strong sense of ownership of the project facilities at the community level.

The purchase of indigenous plants was cost-effective, swift, and the plants had better survival rate due to acclimatization to the local climate. Community involvement—particularly of the women—in protecting treated slide was effective, efficient, and ensured gender mainstreaming.

With improved road quality, many vehicles started to carry goods above the maximum axle-load. Unfortunately, this adversely impacted the sustainability of the roads and should be quickly addressed. Heavy penalties for the violation of axle-load limits could be considered.

Also, given the fiscal constraints and resulting meager operations and maintenance budget, the government could introduce toll collection, at least on the major rehabilitated or reconstructed roads. This would help ensure their sustainability up to the designed life.

3 CARING FOR OUR ENVIRONMENT

COOK ISLANDS: ENERGY WITHIN REACH
Poverty Reduction through Renewable Energy

- → 1,500 people received clean and affordable electricity
- → five island communities gained 100% access to renewable energy

PEOPLE'S REPUBLIC OF CHINA: INNOVATING FOR GREEN FARMING
Integrated Biogas Renewable Energy Sector Development Project

- → people in four provinces enjoyed improved air quality
- → 4.87 million tons of livestock and agricultural waste treated to produce over 126 million cubic meters of biogas, used to generate electricity

▶ 3.1 COOK ISLANDS: ENERGY WITHIN REACH
Poverty Reduction through Renewable Energy

Abstract

The Cook Islands Renewable Energy Sector Project is promoting energy efficiency and renewable energy, increasing access to energy for all, and undertaking reforms to build local capacity and support effective sector governance. The project is cofinanced by ADB, the European Union (which provided the initial funding), the Green Climate Fund, and the Global Environment Facility (subsequent funding). The project is scheduled to complete in December 2022. The initial funding connected solar photovoltaic (PV) and battery storage systems as mini-grids on the small islands of Atiu, Mangaia, Mauke, and Mitiaro, and Aitutaki. This has reduced electricity tariffs and oil imports, delivered more reliable electricity supply, improved living conditions, and created new livelihood opportunities for the island communities. The subsequent funding is being used to install battery storage systems on the capital, Rarotonga, to support higher penetration of intermittent, renewable sources of power into the grid. Overall, the completed part of the project has provided clean and affordable electricity to about 1,500 people—or 9% of the total population—while reducing emissions, creating jobs, and strengthening energy security.

Background

Because of its small size, the Cook Islands' economic development is constrained by the country's distance from markets, lack of resources, and limited infrastructure. The country relies on tourism for about 60% of gross domestic product (GDP). More than 28% of the total population lives below the national poverty line.

The country's outer islands experience even more limited economic opportunities because of their distance from the capital, Rarotonga. About

Project at a Glance

Poverty Reduction through Renewable Energy

Approved:	21 November 2014
Closed:	31 December 2022
Project Cost:	

a. **Initial Financing**

- European Union
  $7.26 million
- Asian Development Bank
  $11.19 million

b. **Additional Financing Global Environment**

- Facility Grant
  $4.26 million
- Green Climate Fund
  $12.00 million

Executing Agency:
Ministry of Finance and Economic Management, Cook Islands

25% of the population lives in these outer islands, where they rely on pineapple processing as a non-tourism commercial activity. This, however, is declining because of competition from cheaper exports. The outer islands have beautiful and pristine environments. However, the Southern group in particular, Atiu, Mangaia, Mauke, and Mitiaro suffer from low tourist arrivals. They are isolated, lack transport services, and have inadequate infrastructure and limited power supply resulting in high electricity costs.

The Cook Islands used to rely heavily on imported fossil fuel as the main source of energy. Fuel imports in 2012 cost $29.8 million, equivalent to 25% of all imports and 9% of GDP. In 2013, reliance on imported fuel—paired with distance from major markets and associated high import costs—led to electricity tariffs

Sign at the entrance of solar PV power station in Mauke, outer islands in the Southern group of the Cook Islands (photo by Eun young So).

averaging $0.63 per kilowatt-hour (kWh), among the highest rates in the world. As a result, electricity costs took up 4% of annual household expenditures, and 15% of annual business expenditures, stunting economic growth, and significantly affecting living standards.

Diesel generators supplied about 99% of total electricity generation capacity in 2012. They were dirty, noisy, and inefficient. Their operation, maintenance, and replacement costs were high. Island administration committees operated and maintained the generators, but had limited technical knowledge. Lack of capacity, particularly on the outer islands, meant energy systems were running inefficiently and unsustainably. Furthermore, the diesel systems were overused and broke down frequently—at times degrading within 5 years, against the expected 30-year operational life span.

Interventions

ADB has assisted by installing solar systems to meet electricity demand with cleaner and more cost-effective resources (ADB 2014).

The project's initial funding built a combined 2.5 megawatt (MW) peak of solar PV and 7.5 megawatt-hour (MWh) of battery energy storage for mini-grids on the five islands, and improved energy sector capacity. These solar systems were completed in October 2019. The subsequent funding involves installing two battery energy storage systems of 2 MW/8 MWh and 6 MW/3 MWh on Rarotonga, to allow more renewable energy generation to be added in the future; and building capacity of locals to operate and maintain batteries. The battery systems under construction in Rarotonga will enable the private sector to build an additional 6 MW peak solar power generation system. This will further reduce generation costs and consumer tariffs.

Because of the country's exposure to disasters, all the new systems have been designed with robust materials to increase their resilience to cyclones and other extreme weather events. Climate-resilient design features are important for maintaining the availability of core services such as health, electricity and water supply, sanitation, and emergency shelters, which are essential for the self-sufficiency of remote islands.

Results

Today, residents of the outer islands have access to 24-hour electricity. They enjoy better living standards and new economic opportunities. Women can work longer hours to make handicrafts, while kids can study in quieter environments without being disturbed by noisy diesel generators. Residents have expanded access to information and communication technology including computers, radio, television, the internet, and cellphones. And they increasingly use electric appliances for income-generating activities such as producing coconut oil, sauce, and jam from local produce (ADB 2020b).

Rangi Kimiora, a baker from Mitiaro island, used to face regular blackouts and power turning off at 12 noon every day in order to save the diesel fuel. Now, with the solar mini-grids on Mitiaro, he is able to bake at any time to provide fresher bread to customers.

With 100% access to renewable energy, all five island communities have opportunities to boost tourism, their key economic sector. This helps attract eco-friendly, high-end tourists interested in sustainable travel.

The project has reduced fuel imports and lowered energy tariffs. The Cook Islands imported 5 million less liters of fuel in 2019 than in 2012, saving $6.9 million on fuel imports. This change brought down the power tariff from $0.63 per kWh to $0.47 per kWh for residential and $0.41 per kWh for commercial consumers as of June 2020.

The project has created jobs, which helps its sustainability. The initial project phase employed 40 local people, of which 25% were women.

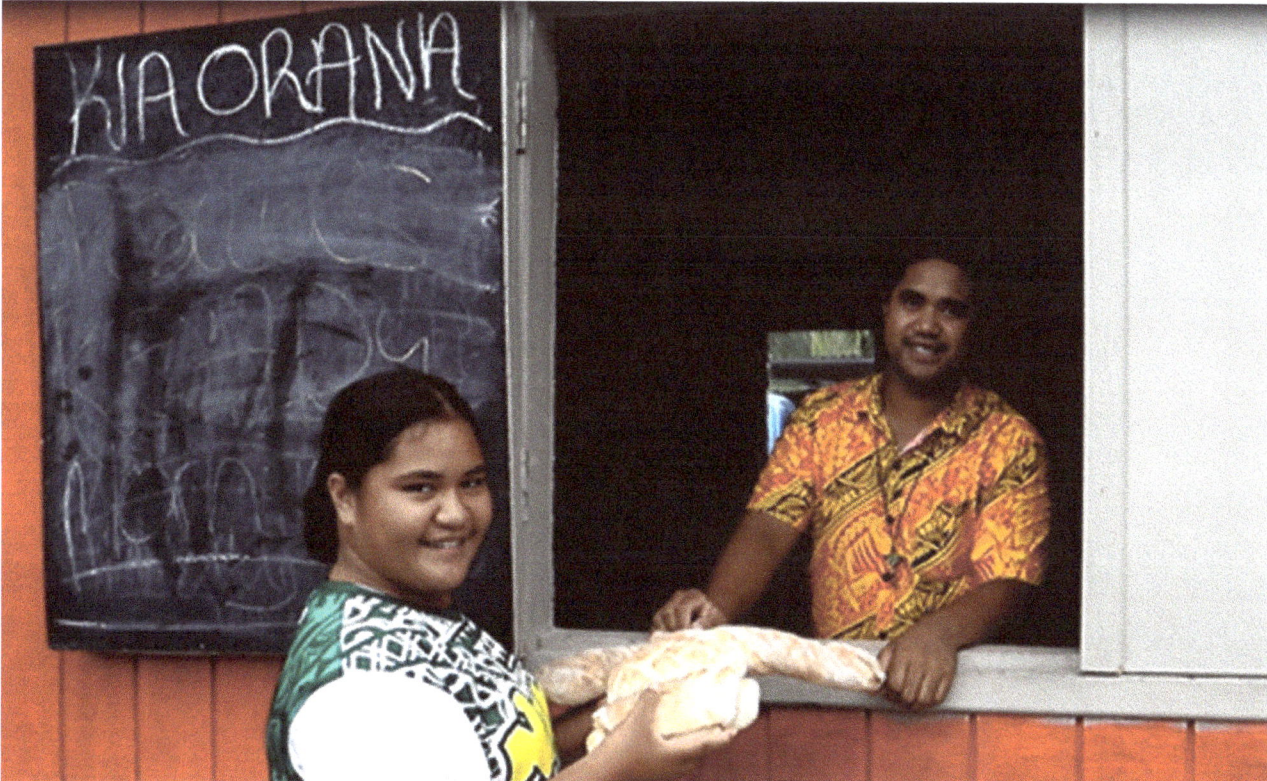

Rangi Kimiora, a baker from Mitiaro island, can now provide freshly baked bread to customers any time of the day without power interruptions (photo by ADB).

Local workers' knowledge, skills, and experience have served the communities well. Several local employees have gone on to continue careers in the energy sector.

The Cook Islands now have lower emissions by 960 tons of carbon dioxide per year. This supports the nation in achieving its climate commitments under the United Nations Framework Convention on Climate Change. The anticipated addition of a 6 MW peak solar array on Rarotonga—made possible by the addition of battery storage under the project—will further reduce emissions.

Lessons Learned

This project is aligned with the government's commitment and supported the Southern Island group to be 100% powered by renewable energy. However, Rarotonga and Aitutaki islands are still making efforts to achieve these targets. The government's ambitious plan will require further progressive planning and implementation, including distributed generation, advanced control and integration, and sophisticated commercial structures.

The project has been successful because of the close consultations with and support of the community. These help ensure alignment with local traditions, deepen community ownership, and ensure sustainable results. Detailed planning for logistics of goods and works is crucial to properly serve the remote outer islands. Local staff have to be properly trained given that this is the first time they work on an energy project.

Battery energy storage is essential to absorb fluctuations in solar power systems which has not only helped maximize the utilization of the renewable power, but also lower the cost of power by reduced consumption of diesel.

The extended hours of power supply with renewables has created new businesses, and allowed existing businesses to operate longer. All this boosts economic activity and income, and contributes to improved quality of life.

The tariff decline has been notable in the outer islands where renewable energy is provided. However, the price at $0.40 per kWh is still high relative to international prices. Thus, increasing the share of renewable energy in the generation mix will contribute to further lowering the tariff for the country.

3.2 PEOPLE'S REPUBLIC OF CHINA: INNOVATING FOR GREEN FARMING
Integrated Biogas Renewable Energy Sector Development Project

Abstract

The Integrated Biogas Renewable Energy Sector Development Project was approved by ADB on 26 March 2010 for $66.08 million. The Global Environmental Facility and the Clean Energy Fund under the Clean Energy Financing Partnership Facility provided grant support of $12.2 million. The project aimed to improve rural livelihood through innovative methods by converting livestock waste to biogas renewable energy, and eco-farming services and products. More than 40% of the subprojects were in both national and provincial poverty counties in Heilongjiang, Henan, Jiangxi, and Shandong provinces in the People's Republic of China (PRC). One of the subproject enterprises, Wannianxinxing, a private owner, implemented a closed loop circular economy where biogas-generated electricity was used by the enterprise, and also sold to the grid with feed-in-tariff. In addition, biogas sludge was converted to organic fertilizer for eco-farming and sale of organic products.

Background

In the PRC, rising rural energy consumption and environmental degradation have been a cause of concern. From 2000 to 2016, rural areas saw an increase in annual energy consumption per person of 9.81% (ADB 2020c). Reliance on coal consumption and burning of straw in rural areas resulted in serious rural to urban transboundary pollutions and negatively impacted climate change. Against this backdrop, the project aimed to utilize livestock waste in rural areas to enable a wider access to biogas renewable energy for improving rural environmental management. It also aimed to achieve resource recycling to advance the ecological civilization agenda in the PRC.

Project at a Glance

Integrated Biogas Renewable Energy Sector Development Project

Approved:	16 April 2010
Closed:	1 September 2020

Project Cost:

- **Clean Energy Fund**
  $3.00 million
- **Global Environment Facility Grant**
  $9.20 million
- **Asian Development Bank**
  $66.08 million

Executing Agencies:
Department of Agriculture, Heilongjiang Province
Department of Agriculture, Henan Province
Department of Agriculture, Foreign Office of Jiangxi Province
Department of Agriculture, Shandong Province

Interventions

The project adopted an integrated approach—it supported livestock industry to reduce nonpoint source of pollutions, built linkage with eco-farming for animal waste residual utilization, and generated renewable biogas energy for electricity consumption to deliver the goal of circular economy.

In the first intervention, 65 medium and large-sized biogas plants (MLBGPs) and six centralized biogas plants were built. These provided 80% energy source of each livestock farm or agro-enterprise. The installed methane capture device reduced greenhouse gas emissions about 95% of the time.

Control and monitoring device for biogas renewable energy negation (photo by ADB).

Second, biogas sludge (a byproduct from the biogas plants) was used to promote eco-farming. The provinces of Heilongjiang, Henan, Jiangxi, and Shandong completed a total of 24,787 *mu* of eco-farming.[2] About 85% of biogas plants supplied biogas sludge to nearby farms as organic fertilizer for fruits, vegetables, and crops. Farmers used more than 1.14 cubic meters (m^3) of biogas slurry and 147,500 tons of biogas residue annually, which reduced the use of chemical fertilizer and pesticide by more than 60%.

Third, through capacity building, farmers were provided guidelines on how to establish centralized biogas plants. They were trained on performance monitoring system for the design and operations of MLBGPs, and the business model for centralized biogas plants. Four provincial technical service centers were established, and about 320 technicians were trained in operations and maintenance of biogas plants.

A case worth highlighting was Wannianxinxing, a private enterprise that overcame the most challenging hurdle in the biogas sector in the PRC. Through the use of biogas from pig manure, its annual power generation reached

about 2.7 million kilowatt-hours (kWh). The enterprise was able to sell this electricity to the local grid at CNY0.75/kWh. To cover the enterprise's electricity consumption, the owner purchased additional electricity from the local grid at CNY0.65/kWh. This ensured stability of utility supply in its entire manufacturing and production process.

Wannianxinxing demonstrated a successful closed loop economy where livestock manure was converted to income-generating opportunities in tackling climate change mitigation and adaptation. Biogas-generated electricity was used by the enterprise, and also sold to the grid with feed-in-tariff. Biogas sludge was converted to organic fertilizer for eco-farming and sale of organic products. Biogas eco-farming meanwhile enhanced the soil quality, which increased agricultural productivity and made carbon sink possible.

Results

Following the interventions, people in the four provinces enjoyed improved air quality. They now relied less on coal-burning for electricity supply and firewood for cooking and heating.

[2] 1 *mu* = 666.67 m^2.

The resulting annual reduction of 1.72 million tons of carbon dioxide was more than twice the target and equivalent to the reduction of methane emissions from livestock farms. About 4.87 million tons of livestock and agricultural waste was treated to produce over 126 million m³ biogas, which was used to generate electricity.

Biogas-related jobs, and the production and sales of organic fertilizers and products contributed to higher income of over 36,000 farming households. More than 3,000 residents worked during project construction with almost half of them female. Each earned an average of CNY32,562. Later, about 1,450 worked in the operations and maintenance of central biogas plants and MLBGPs. More than 800 were female. Their salaries ranged from CNY1,500 to CNY3,500 per month.

The communities became more aware on how to protect the environment. And people started to enjoy safer crops and vegetables. Over 1.48 million tons of biogas slurry manure was used to produce organic fertilizer in 97,672 mu farmlands. This benefited over 16,000 rural households in 281 villages, reducing their spending on chemical fertilizers and increasing their income through better quality agricultural products.

Lessons Learned

The use of biogas in rural areas of the PRC proved a circular economy's viability in tackling climate change. Optimizing biogas-oriented economic solutions with higher-value products was key in enabling a circular economy in the rural livestock industry.

On-grid connection and feed-in-tariff of distributed energy resources such as biogas renewable energy benefited from strong policy support and coordination by local government agents and the local grid.

The business model delivered by Wannianxinxing proved to be economically viable and contributed to rural poor's income generation and job opportunities. It also provided wider environmental, health, and social benefits. The owner's close collaboration with the state grid and local government agencies, and the assurance that distributed energy resources would not cause any external shock to the local grid, were crucial to the success.

Power generator units (photo by ADB).

4 SECURING FOOD FOR ALL

PEOPLE'S REPUBLIC OF CHINA: PURSUING ECOLOGICAL CHANGE FOR ALL

Ningxia Integrated Ecosystem and Agriculture Development Project

→ 6,900 households' livelihoods improved through value chains in agrobusiness
→ 1,734 poor households engaged in ecotourism

BANGLADESH: BROADENING HORIZONS FOR INCREASED INCOMES

Second Crop Diversification Project

→ 19-percentage-point increase in women farmers' landownership
→ 65% increase in farmers' annual income from 2013 to 2016

▶ 4.1 PEOPLE'S REPUBLIC OF CHINA: PURSUING ECOLOGICAL CHANGE FOR ALL
Ningxia Integrated Ecosystem and Agriculture Development Project

Abstract

In August 2008, ADB approved a $100 million loan and the Global Environment Facility provided a $4.5 million grant to revive damaged ecosystems and improve livelihoods of local farmers in Ningxia Hui Autonomous Region, the People's Republic of China (PRC). At project completion in 2016, 2,600 hectares (ha) of land used water-saving irrigation for high-value crops, and 2,299 ha successfully used a "no-tillage" agriculture conservation practice. Improved livelihoods were provided to about 6,900 households through value chains involvement in agrobusiness. A total of 3,300 ha wetlands were rehabilitated, and 1,734 poor households engaged in ecotourism. Technical capacity and environmental awareness of local farmers were strengthened through farmer field schools.

Background

Ningxia is one of the PRC's five ethnic minority regions, with approximately 2.1 million Hui Muslim in 2018, about 36% of the provincial total population. It is mostly a dry and desert-like region and is one of the most underdeveloped and poorest provinces. Its per capita GDP was 79% of the national average, and 6.2% of its population lived below the national poverty line in 2008.

Rural livelihoods are largely dependent on agriculture and horticulture activities. With low incomes, rural farmers have limited opportunities to improve conditions of traditional crops. They tend to expand cropping areas by converting dry land to irrigation and increasing the intensity of land use through agrichemicals for weed, pest, and disease control. As a result,

Project at a Glance		
Ningxia Integrated Ecosystem and Agriculture Development Project		
Approved:	29 August 2008	
Closed:	28 October 2016	
Project Cost:		

- **Global Environment Facility Grant**
  $4.55 million
- **Asian Development Bank**
  $100.00 million

Executing Agency:
Ningxia Finance Bureau, the PRC

approximately 30% of its land is degraded, while its surface and ground water quality has elevated phosphate and nitrogen levels. Without job opportunities, many residents had to leave to work in urban cities. About 60% of the existing Yinchuan Plain population face a future of static or declining income.

Interventions

In 2008, ADB implemented an integrated ecosystem project to improve rural incomes by linking rural farmers to value chains through the cultivation of high-value crops, animal husbandry, and ecotourism (ADB 2018). The project comprised four interventions: (i) land and water resource management, (ii) rural livelihood improvements, (iii) ecosystem conservation, and (iv) integrated ecosystem capacity building and project management.

The first intervention involved land and water resource management. Water-saving irrigation was introduced to 2,600 ha of high-value crops, such as grapes, wolfberry, and Chinese dates. In addition, the "no-tillage practice" for growing and producing fodder and silage was introduced in three conservation agriculture sites of 2,299 ha. Four research programs were also implemented to test new measures for soil nutrient.

The second intervention aimed to improve rural livelihoods. Altogether, about 6,900 rural households were connected to lead agricultural businesses in (i) vineyard growing and management, (ii) dairy farms, (iii) cattle breeding and production, and (iv) plantation and management of shelterbelts and cash trees. These linked local farmers—who either owned the lands or were contracted to farm the lands—to state farms.

For vineyards, 2,400 ha of vineyards were setup with an associated winemaking capacity of 10,000 tons per year. Over 1,000 rural households learned to manage and grow grapes, which provided around 50,000 days of temporary jobs. They earned an average wage of CNY80 ($12) per day. For dairy farms, 20,000 milk cows were bought. Breeding and milking facilities were constructed, and a biodigester (to convert animal waste to supply electricity to the farms) was installed. About 800 locals were employed earning an average monthly salary of CNY4,000—30% higher than the provincial average. In addition, about 30,000 locals were engaged in growing forage including silage and alfalfa. For cattle breeding and production, 10 feedlots for finishing livestock were built, and 1,000 cattle purchased. About 3,900 rural households were employed. Each earned about CNY1,000 for breeding a cattle. The program benefited others beyond the project areas in Xiji county, Yuanzhou district in Guyuan City—one of the poorest areas in the PRC. For shelterbelt management, 750 households were provided free young tress for ecological shelterbelts (190 ha) and cash trees (380 ha).

The third intervention rehabilitated 3,300 ha of wetlands and restored five major lakes, which provided significant ecological services such

as biodiversity and ecotourism. Facilities were also established for environmental and wetland public education in Yuehai and Shahu lakes. Over 1,700 poor households were engaged in project activities including growing aquatic plants, harvesting reeds, farming, raising duck and goose, and tourism services. From 2008 to 2016, the number of tourists to these lakes increased by 161.4%, from 0.93 million to 2.44 million.

In the fourth intervention, a training-of-trainers program including its syllabus was developed to build a pool of experts in grape growing, irrigation and fertigation, dairy farm management, and wetland protection. Staff from agrobusiness companies of the state farm, a major implementing agency of the project, were enrolled in the program. They served as core technical resources for surrounding farms and communities

A vineyard manager shows the soil testing and monitoring instruments, which decide when and how much water and fertilizer are supplied to the vines. The instruments are helpful for growing high-quality grapes (photo by ADB).

Modern dairy farms and beef cattle breeding lots, where local households or farmers are engaged. Lead farms provide technical services, which ensure quality and environmental standards (photo by ADB).

especially in the two farmer field schools. The schools were set up to teach local farmers in grape growing and vineyard management, and cow breeding and dairy farm management.

Results

The project helped 150,000 rural people transit to higher-value agrobusiness. It targeted poor rural communities, especially ethnic smallholders. Rural communities benefited from vocational and technical trainings provided by the farmer field schools. Nonfarming jobs were created in livestock, perennial crops, and other agricultural industries. The number of project beneficiaries grew by 5.3 times to 104,120 people in 2016 from 2009, of which 40% were Hui minority people.

Per capita income of rural farmers grew in the range of 10.4% to 15.0% per year from 2008 to 2016. The average per capita income of project beneficiary households rose by 175% from 2009 to 2015, compared to the 160% growth in control groups.

During the project implementation, local residents worked for 415,000 person-days earning a daily wage between CNY80 to CNY130. Over half of the work went to female laborers, who enjoyed equivalent wages to those of male workers.

The water-saving irrigation system saved more than 30 million cubic meters (m^3) of water per year. Water use in vineyards reduced by 70%. Electricity consumption was also reduced by 70%, saving 3,100 kilowatt-hours (kWh)/ha per year. Fertilizer used was reduced by about 70%. Over 6,000 associated households improved their water use and fertilizer application.

Lessons Learned

The project was effective in reducing poverty for several reasons. First, it linked rural farmers' livelihoods to value chains, which provided stable and increased income from higher-value agrobusiness, such as, dairy farms, beef cattle breeding, and winemaking. As the farmers' agricultural skills improved, their environmental awareness also improved through training provided by the agrobusiness companies. These further strengthened their capabilities to earn more.

Second, ecological benefits were secured by improvements in rural livelihoods. Significant saving in water use and fertilizer application reduced agricultural costs, and improved the quality of agricultural products and their prices. This motivated local farmers to apply more sustainable land and water management practices.

Third, the project promoted community participation during implementation. End users were engaged in project construction works, such as, plantation, small-scale irrigation, and digester, which they also managed upon completion. This enhanced their ownership and improved the quality and maintenance efficiency of the facilities.

Fourth, the project built strong partnerships between agrobusiness companies with local farmers through sustainable capacity building. The farmer field schools and trainers developed through training of trainers ensured continuous training of local farmers, which in turn ensured a high-level of service standards and production expertise in the value chains.

▶ 4.2 BANGLADESH: BROADENING HORIZONS FOR INCREASED INCOMES
Second Crop Diversification Project

Abstract

The Second Crop Diversification Project approved by ADB in 2010 for $40 million, aimed to reduce the poverty of small farmers, including women farmers, in 52 *upazilas* (subdistricts) of 27 districts in the southwest and northwest regions of Bangladesh. The strategy was to encourage farmers to diversify to high-value crops (HVC) for higher incomes. The Government of Bangladesh and BRAC, a nongovernment organization, organized public awareness campaigns; formed small farmers groups; and provided hands-on trainings such as production of high-value crops, business development, credit management, and climate change adaptation. The Bangladesh Bank, through two banks and BRAC, provided credit support. The Local Government Engineering Department established on-farm-small-scale infrastructures, where farmers could sell their produce. The project fostered women's participation through orientation on women's rights and issues affecting women's access to opportunities. Post-project survey showed increases in (i) small farmers' income from increased crop production; (ii) landowning women farmers to 70% from 51% before the project; (iii) women's participation in decision-making in homestead gardening to 40.2% from 10.5%, and in the selection of market to 29% from 8.9%; (iv) women farmers' involvement in HVC production; and (v) women (184 in total) becoming board members of 92 on-farm infrastructures.

Background

Land is Bangladesh's most basic resource, with more than 75% of the population directly or indirectly engaged in agriculture (ADB 2010a). The northwest and southwest regions are the

Project at a Glance	
Second Crop Diversification Project	
Approved:	30 June 2010
Closed:	23 July 2018
Project Cost:	

- **Asian Development Bank**
  $40 million

Executing Agency:
 Bangladesh Bank
 Department of Agricultural Extension

poorest and most backward regions of the country. These regions are physically isolated. They have limited agriculture development, and lack diverse or appropriate crops, information on markets, and market potentials for nontraditional crops. Small, particularly women, farmers find it difficult to access credit.

Rice is a dominant crop contributing to self-sufficiency in food grains and hence food security. But it has resulted in dependency on imported food, particularly HVC, including fruits, vegetables, pulses, and spices, which the poor cannot afford. As such, increasing HVC production is critical to reducing imports, and enhancing the affordability and nutritious diets of the poor.

Interventions

This project followed the successful ADB-assisted Northwest Crop Diversification Project completed in June 2009. It complemented the earlier project and other ADB supports, by promoting value addition to HVCs, and strengthening value-chain integration by developing backward and forward linkages between farmers and consumers.

■ Women beneficiaries in Jessore District, Khulna Division during a consultation meeting with representatives from the project evaluation team and the Department of Agricultural Extension (photo by ADB).

It included service provisions by private sector agribusinesses, microfinance institutions, and wholesale banks.

The project focused on forward-looking, but resource-poor and less well-served small, marginal, and medium-sized farmers. The first intervention involved supporting the farmers' transition to HVC through awareness campaigns, trainings, and access to market. To encourage farmers to diversify to HVC, the Department of Agricultural Extension (DAE), the project executing and implementing agency, with the support of BRAC conducted public awareness campaigns and encouraged the farmers to organize. ADB helped develop the campaigns and criteria for selection of farmer groups particularly in relation to women's participation. Altogether, over 250,00 farmers, of whom more than half were women, formed 12,000 small groups. Some of these groups had women members only.

Farmers received hands-on training in the production of HVCs which included integrated pest management techniques; reduced and zero tillage practices; green and organic manure application; and controlled environment agricultural technology and mechanization for cultivation, harvesting, and postharvest handling. These were carried out through lectures and field-based training, demonstration plots, cross-field learning, motivational tours, agriculture fairs, and extension services. Farmers were also trained in organizational and leadership development, business development, credit management, bargaining, and climate change adaptation.

To link farmers to HVC markets and traders through on-farm-small-scale infrastructures, over 100 farmer marketing associations with 1,955 farmers, of whom 30% were women, were formed. The latter were established by the Local Government Engineering Department with DAE and relevant local level authority.

ADB developed the criteria and monitored the formation of the associations to ensure that they were well represented by women. ADB also helped link farmers to large external, district, and nearby markets.

To enable farmers to purchase required inputs, financing was channeled through Bangladesh Bank to BRAC, which was disbursed to farmer groups. By 2017, BRAC had disbursed credit support of Tk8,631.8 million (over $100 million), including revolving funds. This was 400% of the target, and the number of farmers reached was 120% of the target. Three years after the project was completed, the total credit disbursed reached Tk19,765.50 million ($232.5 million), of which 61% went to women. In total, 205,989 HVC farmers—123,909 (60%) women—received credit support through BRAC.

Farmers bought high-quality planting materials from nurseries of the Horticulture Development Training Center, which was refurbished and upgraded through ADB financing. The materials supported a range of high-value fruits, vegetables, pulses, spices, cut flowers, potted plants, and foliage production; added value to coconuts, through coir and virgin coconut oil production; and promoted profitable farming systems through intercropping and other environment-friendly activities.

ADB support enabled the construction of 92 on-farm-small-scale infrastructures to reduce postharvest losses and improve the quality of produce. Farmers also funded a smaller share of the construction cost. These infrastructures were on-farm (or near-farm) collection and postharvest handling centers, including washing, drying, sorting, grading, and packaging facilities; and small-scale cool, cold, and dry storage and market-related transport facilities.

To foster women's participation, DAE and a nongovernment organization oriented farmer groups on women's rights, and helped women address social issues affecting their access to opportunities such as child and women's health, sanitation, acid-throwing on women, early marriage, dowry, and divorce.

Results

The project transformed cropping practices and boosted income. The successful HVC production with new technology attracted farmers to shift to HVC production. The adoption of HVC increased cropping intensity by 34.27%, mainly due to triple cropping by many farmers. HVC production was helped by $232.5 million credit disbursed to targeted farmers.

Overall, farmers' annual income increased by 65% from 2013 to 2016, which was significantly higher than the target of 20%. Fruit farmers saw their annual income increased by 25.7% versus pre-project income; vegetable farmers, 86.7%; and spice farmers, 26.5%. From HVC production such as tomato, onion, and brinjal, in only 0.167 ha of land (0.41 acre), a marginal farmer with land size below 0.49 acre could earn a net income of around Tk75,000.

Said Fatima Begum, 47, a widow with 17-year-old son: "I used to work as a day laborer in other people's land. I weed, harvest, and husk. For this work, I receive Tk250–Tk300 per day. Through the project, I attended skills training in high-value crop production (vegetables). After the training, I started to grow traditional soil potato, spinach, beans on the roof, string beans, and chickpeas, and raise goats in my homestead land. The training taught me to call the local level livestock officer if my goats get sick. From vegetable production and goat-raising, I earn and able to save Tk20,000, which I use to meet for my family's nutrition needs and my son's education expenses. I want to see my son to be an agricultural graduate, employed, and working like the agriculture officers. Now, I know whom to talk to and which departments to approach in case of problems with my livestock and homestead gardening, and more importantly, local people know about my ability to work."

■ Selina Begum wraps a flower head with a netting cap to help it grow into an ideal shape and protect it from pests (photo by ADB).

More landless agricultural laborers found jobs. Cultivation of HVCs required about 20% higher labor input for better land preparation, fertilizer application, irrigation, harvesting, and postharvest operations. Since HVCs were grown throughout the year, more labor was required during the lean period. The additional 93,870 ha land cultivated with HVCs meant more work for the poor landless workers. This increased labor demand brought more work to women agricultural workers—from 47,880 days to 61,320 days for crop cultivation, from 21,520 days to 34,620 days for postharvest (processing, storing) activities, and from 5,180 days to 8,160 days for marketing—which increased women's income.

More women were empowered. Some women became landowners, an exception given the cultural barriers of women owning land in Bangladesh. Women's mobility also increased. Women could now access hospitals for their health concerns, and easily go to the markets to purchase essentials.

Food consumption and the diet of the beneficiaries improved. Frequency of daily food intake was significantly higher for the farmer-beneficiaries than the non-beneficiaries (85.14% versus 75.91%). Food intake with rich menu increased from 15.29% to 19.52% in 3-4 times weekly. Food security through reliance on own production increased from 15.77% to 20.87%; and among the beneficiaries, 87.4% had no food shortage. Finally, food surplus increased from 15% to 20% of households, and food deficit decreased from 18.32% to 10.43% of households.

"My training in cultivating climate-resilient high-value crops helped me obtain an agricultural loan of Tk15,000 from BRAC. My husband and I used the loan to grow vegetables in his land for income. For the repayment of the loan, both of us agreed to share equal responsibility, which relieved me of extra mental stress. We use our income for our children's education and family food security and nutrition and to buy a TV for recreation. Me and my husband dream of a better life for our son and daughters," said Chandana Biswas, 34, mother of three children.

With increased income, farmer ownership of resources also increased. Farmer ownership in power tiller went up by 38.3%; thresher, 92.1%; and shallow tube well, 32.8%. Meanwhile the rate of sanitation increased from 48.4% to 62.12%, ownership of tub well from 84.8% to 90.9%, and use of electricity from 56.5% to 60%.

Environment impact improved. Around 74% of farmers practiced organic farming, which increases soil fertility and production, minimizes pest infestation, and decreases production cost. Farmers are also now more aware of adaptation of climate-resilient crops and varieties.

Lessons Learned

The combination of capacity development on HVC production, marketing, and networking through various trainings, workshops, exchange visits, demonstrations, and credit support helped farmers achieve sustained income, thus lifting them out of poverty.

Several lessons could be learned from the project. The importance of establishing a transparent accreditation certification for product traceability, and crop zoning to enhance location-specific crops to overcome supply glut was brought out. In addition, adequate storage facilities for temporary storing of fresh produce was key to reduce postharvest losses.

On-farm-small-scale infrastructures were useful because of their easy accessibility to both farmers and buyers. While training of farmers' marketing associations on business development and management was vital in sustaining their operations.

Local agricultural training institutes provided e-learning tools to enable farmer-trainees to access online training modules either at their homes or in nearby internet shops at their convenience.

5 SUSTAINING PROSPERITY THROUGH ACCESS TO FINANCE

PAPUA NEW GUINEA: CHANGING MINDSETS FOR FINANCIAL INCLUSION
Microfinance Expansion Project
- → 218,000 people received financial education
- → 330,000 new savings accounts opened

NEPAL: WIDENING THE ROAD TO GROWTH
Decentralized Rural Infrastructure and Livelihood Project
- → 42% reduction in transportation cost of people, 80% of goods
- → 552 community infrastructures established

▶ 5.1 PAPUA NEW GUINEA: CHANGING MINDSETS FOR FINANCIAL INCLUSION
Microfinance Expansion Project

Abstract

In late 2010, ADB approved a $25 million project to improve microfinance services in Papua New Guinea (PNG), provide financial literacy and business development skills training, and increase the number of loan and savings accounts held by the population, especially by women and in rural areas. The project, which was implemented from 2011 to mid-2019, achieved all of these objectives and made a significant impact on financial inclusion in PNG. It provided financial education to 218,000 people, business development skills training to 17,000 individuals, 4,500 days of training to staff of microfinance institutions, and facilitated more than 330,000 new savings accounts. The project also promoted innovations in financial products and service delivery and fostered the economic empowerment of women. Through its flagship mass financial literacy program, it put financial inclusion on the development agenda in PNG.

Background

The PNG faces a unique challenge where about 85% of its population live in rural areas, a large proportion of whom have very limited school education and have low literacy and numeracy rates. Most people have never banked with a financial institution (ADB 2010b).

Rose Peter, 43, from Simbu Province is the mother of three schoolchildren. Throughout her life, she never thought of trying to save money for future expenses such as her children's education or emergencies. Many in PNG had similar concerns as only 15% of the population was estimated to have access to formal or informal banking facilities. This percentage was even lower in rural areas.

Project at a Glance		
Microfinance Expansion Project		
Approved:	28 October 2010	
Closed:	30 June 2020	
Project Cost:		

- **Government of Australia**
  $6.09 million
  $6.00 million
- **Asian Development Bank**
  $13.00 million

Executing Agency:
Bank of Papua New Guinea

The microfinance sector in PNG faced other issues apart from lack of access to financial services. Poor financial literacy and business management skills were widespread. Microfinance institutions (MFIs) did not have the capacity to meet the increased borrowing needs of micro and small enterprises (MSEs). There was a lack of a microfinance-specific legal and regulatory framework and accepted industry-wide standards. The demand for microfinance services was believed to be more than twice the available supply.

Interventions

In response to these issues, ADB's Microfinance Expansion Project was implemented to improve the supply and use of financial services, especially in areas outside the capital of Port Moresby and major provincial capitals.

The project's first intervention involved improving the business and product management capacity of MFIs. Specialists and consultants developed the capacity of MFI staff through trainings and business mentoring. The MFI staff were trained on business processes and practices such as risk management; credit (origination, assessment, and approval); liquidity management; lending and credit recoveries; and business operations (including human resources, and improvements in core banking systems and information technologies).

Second, nationwide financial education and business development skill trainings were conducted. People were taught how to manage their money and use financial services. Given the popularity of mobile devices, a mobile banking training module was also introduced to help people access financial services via their devices. Entrepreneurs were also taught business management skills, including how to expand their businesses and obtain credit.

Third, a partial credit guarantee scheme, called "Risk Share Facility," was created and used to increase the amount of MSE lending by MFIs.

Results

The best performing 11 from 21 MFIs were selected to participate in the project. The Institute of Business and Banking Management trained MFI staff in a comprehensive training program that included 16 modules in five locations across PNG, covering over 4,500 days of training. Each MFI had a business mentor, who, for over 3 years supported the implementation of improved accounting, management information systems, reporting, human resources, and operational and business management. Through these the MFIs began to improve and diversify their services to customers.

With the project's support, one of the MFIs—East New Britain Savings and Loan Society—acquired a new core banking system and developed 27 new banking products. Among the nine new products implemented were:

- a loan that targeted individuals involved in the supply chain of small-scale fishing;

- a short-term working capital loan for women to improve their microbusinesses, such as selling ice blocks, secondhand clothes, or cooked food, operating a trade store, sewing, growing vegetables, or managing a taxi service;
- a long-term savings product for clients to build funds for their children's higher education;
- a loan for women to start or improve poultry enterprises;
- a loan to assist women street vendors or selling at main urban markets; and
- a life insurance product for loan recipients.

Now, more than 100,000 women, out of a total of over 200,000 rural inhabitants assisted, know how to manage their money through financial education and business development skill training. The financial education training included information on how to open an account at a financial institution, and 47% of the financial education trainees opened an account following their training. The project contributed to the total number of savings accounts increasing from 187,500 in 2010 to 518,413 by 30 June 2019.

■ Rose Peter learns how to open specific accounts to set aside money for different purposes through the project financial literacy training. (photo by ADB).

■ Financial education course graduates Leap Elijah and Letom Kauip from Tsak Valley, Enga Province (photo by ADB).

Rose Peter, who now sells lime and mustard (*dakar*) in the local market has taken a loan to expand her business with help from her husband. She now makes and sells scones and runs a small general goods store in her village. "Before attending the financial education training, I never ever bothered to save money, but after the training, I opened three accounts: (i) an emergency fund, (ii) a savings and loan account, and (iii) a school fee account. Now I intend to use my money wisely." Rose said she has repaid all her loans. Her businesses are also flourishing. According to Rose, her spending is more focused. She uses her money for her family's needs. "Now I have the knowledge to manage all my expenses and pay my children's school fees." Rose said she now understands the importance of saving.

The Risk Share Facility provided partial credit guarantees to more than 2,000 loans totaling $8 million by four MFIs. Two-thirds of the loans were provided to women. Anecdotal reports from other new clients of microfinance providers noted the positives impacts of having a savings account. They enjoyed not having their life's savings "hidden under the mattress" in cash, and also the new ability to save their hard-earned money to achieve their goals, whether for education, to start a new business, or simply saving "for a rainy day."

Another achievement was the establishment of the Centre for Excellence in Financial Inclusion, responsible for implementing the government's national financial inclusion strategy. Using project funds, the center also developed an innovative financial inclusion mapping tool.

Lessons Learned

Several lessons could be learned from the project. First, low-income people in PNG have a greater demand for savings products than loans. Second, there is a strong interest among low-income people to learn about savings and budgeting. Third, providing useful training to a diverse set of MFIs requires hiring the right consultants. Fourth, contracting the right trainers was difficult and sufficient lead time was needed. Fifth, high turnover of MFI staff meant that training needed to be repeated several times over the life of the project. Lastly, ADB project administration consultancy support was critical because of limited capacity in the government's project management unit.

► 5.2   NEPAL: WIDENING THE ROAD TO GROWTH
Decentralized Rural Infrastructure and Livelihood Project

Abstract

From 2004 to 2017, ADB supported the Decentralized Rural Infrastructure and Livelihood Project of Nepal. The project sought to reduce poverty in conflict-affected communities in 18 hill and mountainous districts by constructing and rehabilitating roads and bridges and improving the people's livelihood. The project constructed a 527-kilometer (km) road network and 422 trail bridges, which lowered the cost of transportation of people by 42% and of goods by 80%. It made social services and economic opportunities more accessible to people in the project areas. The road construction and rehabilitation works provided jobs for over 150,000 members of building groups. To maximize benefits of improved roads, using a community-driven approach, the project established 552 community infrastructures— school buildings, water supply, sanitation, irrigation pond, community electrification, foot trail, health facilities, and village roads. It also trained more than 7,500 people from disadvantaged groups in livelihood skills and connected members of building groups to microfinance institutions. In 2016, the average annual household income in these areas increased by 36%. In 2015, the poverty level in rural areas decreased to 23% from 41% in 2004.

Background

The widespread poverty in the western, eastern, and central districts in Nepal is largely due to the interrelated factors of poor road connectivity, high transport costs, and limited mobility of people. In 2011, only 17% of the rural population had access to an all-weather road network, which constrained access to services and economic opportunities (ADB 2011).

Project at a Glance
Decentralized Rural Infrastructure and Livelihood Project
Approved: 31 October 2011
Closed: 11 September 2019
Project Cost:

- **Asian Development Bank**
  $60.98 million
- **Government of Switzerland**
  $13.96 million
- **OPEC Fund for International Development**
  $20.00 million

Executing Agency:
Department of Local Infrastructure Development and Agriculture Roads, Nepal

In addition, the areas were marred by a decade-long armed conflict from 1996 to 2006, which killed more than 17,000 people across the country, and severely impacted infrastructure development and economic activities. Most affected were the poor and disadvantaged people—people discriminated based on their sex, caste, ethnicity, religion, and geographic location—especially in the hill and mountain districts. They lacked access to economic opportunities, education, and social services. The conflict displaced over 400,000 landowners and directly affected nearly 2.4 million people, mostly in the mid- and far-western region.

Interventions

The project constructed a 527 km earthen road and rehabilitated a 249 km road to an all-weather standard (ADB 2019b). It also built seven motorable bridges, and 422 trail bridges to enhance and increase access to road infrastructure services.

Mason training conducted to the Chepang community under the livelihood skills program. The community represents 0.26% of the total population and is categorized as highly marginalized indigenous people (photo by ADB).

First, to achieve these, a labor-intensive, environment-friendly, and participatory approach was adopted. This provided skilled and semi-skilled jobs in construction to the local population by avoiding the use of heavy construction equipment. Local resources over imported resources were also used. Priority for project jobs was given to the project-affected poor households such as those who lost their land, women, and disadvantaged groups.

The environment-friendly aspects came from the use of less-intrusive manual labor, restriction on blasting, and less-damaging handheld tools such as hammers, chisels, spades, and wheelbarrows. The longer time used for road construction facilitated slope stabilization through natural forces such as rainfall. Also, bioengineering works and adoption of the cut-and-fill approach in construction contributed to slope stabilization and faster growth of vegetation along the road alignment.

To facilitate local participation, various village and district committees, including women and members of disadvantaged groups were formed. They helped decide on places that needed assistance. They helped supervise and monitor, and were involved in road construction, rehabilitation, and maintenance works. For example, the building groups carried out construction activities, and the grievance redress committees attended to project district and subproject grievances. These arrangements helped ensure community engagement, and enrich community ownership. Employment was assured for at least one member of a household in the project area.

To help manage challenges of government-led construction works in conflict-affected areas, the Department of Local Infrastructure Development and Agriculture Roads (DOLIDAR) engaged local nongovernment organizations to conduct awareness-raising campaigns. They also formed and mobilized the building groups, facilitated the delivery of benefits and wages to workers, and monitored the implementation of the project's gender equality and social inclusion action plans.

Second, interventions to enhance the project's economic returns and support community livelihood were carried out. Over 500 community infrastructures were built, such as school and community buildings, small irrigation ponds, water supply and sanitation facilities, electrification projects, mule and foot trails, health facilities, village roads, and market centers.

The project area's poor were taught how to better use the income they received from road construction and rehabilitation works, and in livelihood skills. More than 7,500 members of building groups were trained in livelihood skills. Savings mobilization and credit schemes were organized to ensure that workers retained a portion of their wages to help pay off household debts and invest in small-scale income-generating activities. Eighty-two savings groups from 113 building groups were formed. Their members were trained in savings, credit, and microfinance access. These members saved a total of NRs2.09 million, of which 99% was taken as loans by 231 members for their livelihood projects. These mechanisms helped translate the residents' short-term benefits from employment in project road works into long-term livelihood development and capital formation.

■ Off-season vegetable farming training given to women groups in Chitwan District (photo by ADB).

Results

Rural livelihood improved not only through employment in the roads and community infrastructure construction works, but also through the acquisition of livelihood skills, and access to microfinance, savings and credit schemes, and community infrastructures.

Direct employment, indirect services, and connection to the wider road network contributed to the average annual income per household increase—from NRs69,500 in 2007 to NRs186,312 in 2016, higher than the national average of NRs139,824 (DOLIDAR 2016). Short-term employment in construction works for unskilled labor of 11.90 million person-days were realized. All these went to the poor and disadvantaged groups, of which 36% were women, and 59% of the workers were employed for 90 days a year. Construction workers earned a total of $31.28 million.

Said Geeta Khadka, 20 years old, "I am from an impoverished family in Dhobi, which is a remote mountain village in eastern Nepal. During the construction of a community medical clinic, which was one of the community infrastructures built, I was surprised to learn that I could apply as a construction worker, a job usually reserved for men. They said they would hire a man or a woman, whoever could do the work. As my family needed money for our basic needs, I applied. I also had limited work opportunities because of my lack of education. I cannot read and write. I did simple construction tasks, and I learned to do these tasks from experienced workers. I used my earnings to support my parents and brother. The job gave us the chance to prove that women can do construction work and we are paid the same amount as men. Through this work, I learned construction work and improved my life."

Better roads reduced transportation costs, and increased mobility and access to services. For the first time, two districts (Solukhumbu and Mugu)

were connected to the national strategic road network. The constructed road network and trail bridges provided almost half a million people with better access to social services and economic opportunities. The transportation cost for people decreased by 42%, and for goods by 80%.

With the reduced cost of goods and transportation, market links expanded, and market information and delivery became quicker and faster. Small market centers with retail shops, tea shops, hotels and lodges, and vehicle repair services emerged. These provided residents with access to nearer and better markets to sell their high-value crops at better prices. Local employment and livelihood opportunities were created.

The improved roads increased women's mobility, and employment and business opportunities. Women's leadership skills were developed through trainings and representation in groups, which led some to join in local elections. Savings and credit groups empowered women members and the disadvantaged groups with knowledge on microfinance, fund mobilization, and access to credit.

Khun Maya Roka shared her experience, "I took a 3-month veterinary training under the project. After the training, I wanted to practice my skills, but people in my village discouraged women from doing work associated with men, such as veterinary. It was challenging for me to castrate domesticated animals. Even if livestock farming is one of the livelihood activities in the village and the community badly needed veterinarians, they did not accept me because I am a woman. I was not able to practice my work immediately after the training. What I did was to work as a trainer in veterinary training conducted by different organizations in my village. I trained about 20–25 women. That strengthened my self-confidence. My persistence also led the villagers to accept me as a woman vet. I also started an agro vet shop 6 months ago. The

Through the project-led veterinary training, Khun Maya Roka has established herself as a woman vet in her village. She also runs a vet shop and supports family with her earnings (photo by ADB).

shop is running well. The project road helped shorten the time to reach the market and get medicines and other materials for the shop. I plan to continue my job and train women for this work. I am already supporting my family with my shop's earning."

The surrounding environment benefited from the project. After construction, slopes in road alignments became more stable. There was less disturbance to the natural setting because of the manual work, along with technically engineered slope-cutting, road grade design, and partial application of bioengineering. Upgrading of earthen to gravel roads helped reduce carbon emissions by reducing the use of fossil fuels, as travel times were reduced. There was also less dependency on forests for firewood and timber. Instead, better connectivity contributed to the greater use of liquefied natural gas for cooking, and modern materials for construction.

Lessons Learned

The labor-intensive, environment-friendly, and participatory approach was pivotal to the project's success. Formation of various groups ensured community participation, especially of women and disadvantaged groups, which contributed to strong community ownership.

Short-term employment in construction works, introduction of savings and credit practices, and training in livelihood skills helped diversify and improve residents' economic situations, and in turn reduced poverty.

While the immediate cash inflow and basic skills learned from the project facilitated seasonal labor out-migration, the beneficiaries' added income and new skills acquired through the project should help them in the long run. Through extended skills training, the project can enable sustained economic opportunities.

6 CONCLUSION

Lessons learned from the projects presented in this publication provide helpful solutions in addressing the unfinished development agenda particularly in further reducing poverty in the region.

A key lesson was the importance of the support from the government and stakeholders. The projects were in line with the government's development strategy and sector goals. They considered the needs of different stakeholders—the beneficiaries, government, and private sector. In addition, active community participations provided a strong sense of ownership of the projects. For example, the poor in the mountainous areas of Nepal were involved in the planning, supervision, and monitoring of the project's road works. They were employed in building and maintaining the roads. They worked in community amenities built and operating along the roads, and formed various committees that addressed grievances.

Another lesson was the need for projects to follow an integrated, holistic, and sustainable approach. For example, to raise rural farmers' income in Bangladesh, high-value crops, and more advanced and environment-friendly agricultural practices were promoted. Value-chain integration was also strengthened by developing backward and forward linkages between farmers and markets through a variety of skill trainings, employment, credit, and provision of materials and ingredients. Trainings and capacity building were key in ensuring project sustainability. As farmers' agricultural skills improved, their environmental awareness also improved. This brought further ecological benefits, and further strengthened their capabilities to earn higher income.

Many projects also applied innovative solutions. To address the environmental damage caused by the overreliance on coal and burning of straws for energy in rural areas, the biogas project in Jiangxi Province, the PRC used animal waste from livestock farms to produce biogas for electricity. The electricity was fed back to the livestock farms and sold to the grid. The byproduct (sludge) of the biogas plants was in turn converted to fertilizers and used for eco-farming. This innovative solution created an environmentally and socially sustainable circular economy.

Many of the projects also targeted their support to women, minorities, the vulnerable, and/or the disadvantaged. Women continued to face many challenges in contributing to and benefiting from development. In response, for example, the rural road project in India included numerous features that promoted the empowerment of women and the vulnerable, such as through women's participation in project planning and grievance redressal committees; road-friendly design for the elderly, children, women, and people with disabilities; socially inclusive and gender-responsive training materials; and women's participation in technical and nontechnical rural road capacity development initiatives.

REFERENCES

Asian Development Bank. 2004. *Report and Recommendation of the President on a Proposed Loan and Technical Assistance Grant to the Kingdom of Nepal for the Decentralized Rural Infrastructure and Livelihood Project.* Manila.

———. 2005. *Report and Recommendation of the President to the Board of Directors on a Proposed Loan and Technical Assistance Grant to the People's Republic of Bangladesh for the Agribusiness Development Project.* Manila.

———. 2008. *Country Partnership Strategy: People's Republic of China, 2008–2010.* Manila.

———. 2009. *Mainstreaming Climate Change in ADB's Operations—Regional Department Climate Change Implementation Plan: South Asia—Bangladesh (2009–2011).* Manila.

———. 2010a. *Report and Recommendation of the President to the Board of Directors: Proposed Loan People's Republic of Bangladesh: Second Crop Diversification Project.* Manila.

———. 2010b. *Report and Recommendation of the President to the Board of Directors for the Proposed Loan and Administration of Grant Papua New Guinea: Microfinance Expansion Project.* Manila.

———. 2011. *Report and Recommendation of a Proposed Loan, Grant, and Administration of Loan for Additional Financing to the Government of Nepal for the Decentralized Rural Infrastructure and Livelihood Project.* Manila.

———. 2012a. *India: Rural Connectivity Investment Program. Facility Administration Manual.* Manila.

———. 2012b. *Report and Recommendation of the President to the Board of Directors: Proposed Multitranche Financing Facility, Technical Assistance, and Administration of Technical Assistance to the Government of India for the Rural Connectivity Investment Program. Summary of Poverty Reduction and Social Strategy.* Manila.

———. 2014. *Report and Recommendation of the President to the Board of Directors: Proposed Loan and Administration of Grant Cook Islands: Renewable Energy Sector Project.* Manila.

———. 2015. *Additional Financing: Proposed Administration of Grant Nauru: Electricity Supply Security and Sustainability Project.* Manila.

————. 2015b. *Report and Recommendation of the President to the Board of Directors: Proposed Loan and Technical Assistance Grant Islamic Republic of Pakistan: Flood Emergency Reconstruction and Resilience Project.* Manila.

————. 2018. *Project Completion Report: People's Republic of China—Ningxia Integrated Ecosystem and Agriculture Development Project.* Manila.

————. 2019a. *India Gender Equality Results Case Study—Rural Connectivity Investment Program, Connecting People, Transforming Lives.* Manila.

————.2019b. *Completion Report, Nepal: Decentralized Rural Infrastructure and Livelihood Project.* Kathmandu.

————. 2020a. *Completion Report: India: Rural Connectivity Investment Program—Tranche 1.* Manila.

————. 2020b. *Pacific Energy Update.* Manila.

————. 2020c. *Completion Report: People's Republic of China: Integrated Renewable Biomass Energy Development Sector Project.* Manila.

————. 2021. *Key Indicators for Asia and the Pacific 2021.* Manila.

Bangladesh Rural Advancement Committee Microfinance Institution. 2020. *Crop Report.* February.

Government of Bangladesh, Department of Agricultural Extension, Ministry of Agriculture, Rural Development Academy. 2018. *Second Crop Diversification Project Completion Survey Report.* Bogra.

Government of Nepal. 2002. *10th Five-Year Plan (2002–2007).* Kathmandu.

————. 2008. *Three Year Interim Plan (2008–2010).* Kathmandu.

————. 2011. *12th Three-Year Plan (2011–2013).* Kathmandu.

————. 2014. *13th Plan (2014–2016).* Kathmandu.

————. 2017. *14th Plan (2017–2019).* Kathmandu.

Government of Nepal, Department of Local Infrastructure Development and Agriculture Roads. 2016. *Outcome Monitoring Survey Report FY 2072/73.* Kathmandu.

Nikolic, D. et al. 2016. *Cook Islands: 100% Renewable Energy in Different Guises.* Maldives.

www.ingramcontent.com/pod-product-compliance
Lightning Source LLC
Chambersburg PA
CBHW042035220326
41599CB00045BA/7424

* 9 7 8 9 2 9 2 9 6 9 6 0 9 2 *